DesignOriginals

NOTEBOOK DOODLES®
SUPERSTAR

JESS ♥ VOLINSKI

This book belongs to:

you are BEAUTIFUL!

DESIGN ORIGINALS
an Imprint of Fox Chapel Publishing
www.d-originals.com

Be YOURSELF to be creative

The thing I love most about art—making it myself or enjoying others' creations—is that **art allows you to be yourself by expressing yourself.** Whatever you love, whatever is important to you, whatever makes you who you are should come out in your art. By making art that matters to you, you're starting a conversation with everyone who sees it. You're saying, "Hey! This matters to me. What do **you** think about it?"

You might be wondering, how exactly do I express myself with art? That's where **The Elements of Art** come in. You might remember these from art class. Just like writers use words to tell a story, artists use these visual elements to express themselves and start their art conversation. All visual art—whether it is a painting in a museum, storyboards for a movie, a pattern on a bag, or a coloring book page—uses some combination of these seven basic building blocks of art. Not all art has to include all seven elements, but most art will include a few.

The Elements of Art

A **line** is formed as the connected distance between two points. Lines can be thick or thin, straight or curved.

Space refers to the areas in a piece of art that are around or within different parts of the art. There are two kinds of space: negative (space around areas), and positive (space within areas).

A **shape** is a defined area of space—a circle, square, blob, or a flower petal are all shapes.

Texture refers to the way the art physically feels when touched, or how an artist visually makes the art **look** like it would feel. Shading with pencils is an example of this type of visual texture.

Something has **form** if it has volume (or creates the illusion of volume). A three-dimensional sculpture has form. A two-dimensional drawing with shading that makes it appear three-dimensional can also have form.

Color is created when light hits an object and is reflected to our eyes. A color can be described with three properties: hue (the color's name, such as "red"), value (how light or dark the color is, also called a tint or shade of the color), and intensity (how vivid or dull the color is).

Value refers to the relationship between light areas and dark areas in a piece of art.

The Elements of art IN ACTION

Let's look at one of my doodles and see what Elements of Art are here. Even though this is just a simple black and white drawing, it has line, shape, and space. When you color it in, you'll probably add form, color, value, and maybe even texture. That's all seven Elements of Art—on a coloring book page! How cool is that?! Art truly is all around us!

Space (negative): The shape inside the curl is a negative space.

Shape

Line

Space (positive): The shape of this curl creates a positive space.

Texture

Form (and texture): The colored pencil texture makes the star look three-dimensional, giving it form.

Color

Value (dark)

Value (light)

Coloring Technique Ideas

Watercolors

Colored pencils layered over watercolors

Fine-point black pen layered over markers

Get inspired by COLOR

When it comes to expressing emotion, I think color is probably the most powerful Element of Art. To me, there's no better way to express how you're feeling, or how you want someone else to feel, than through the use of color. Just think of some of your favorite memories and how they make you feel. I bet color plays a big part of what you remember. Whether it's a beautiful sunset, the green of spring after a long, cold winter, or a perfectly clean, white expanse of snow, color makes a huge impact on us, both visually and emotionally. Just look at the way different colors can give the same flower drawing a completely different feel.

I've found that planning is key when working with color. If you're like me and you just **love** color, it might seem a bit overwhelming to get started. There are just so many color choices! And it's easy to fall into the rut of using the same colors over and over again, just because you like them. Making color decisions before you start can make you feel comfortable using new colors. Plus, you won't have to make a choice when you're in the midst of coloring and decide you don't like the result as much as you thought you would. A great way to try some new color combinations is to take a few minutes—it won't take long!—to create your own palettes before you get started.

Here's a fun trick I've learned for making palettes. It works especially well if you're using markers or colored pencils. Lay out all of your markers (or pencils) on a table or floor so you can see every single color you have. Pick one favorite marker (pencil) that will serve as the **anchor color** for your palette. Make it a color you really enjoy working with (or for a challenge, maybe a color you never work with). Now, pick two or three other markers (pencils) that complement your anchor color and place those next to your anchor color to start building a palette. Keep going until you have picked five or six colors. At this point, you don't even have to use them—you're just putting them side-by-side to see how the colors look together. Keep adding or switching colors until you like what you see. It's so easy to swap different colors in and out this way. Once you have a group of colors that you like, test them out on paper to make sure you still like the way they look together. If you love it, be sure to create a sample page with the names of the markers/colors you used so you won't forget. This is a great way to quickly create a whole library of color palettes for yourself.

Another great place to get color inspiration is literally from the world around you. Color is everywhere—your clothing, your bag, even a tissue box—there are probably patterns and designs with interesting color palettes surrounding you now! I'm sure there are things you bought because you liked the colors, so use those things that you love as inspiration. I once bought a pack of hair elastics simply because they had the most beautiful combination of blues and purples. Almost anything, anywhere, can become a color inspiration, so always keep your eyes open!

A SPECTRUM of Emotion

Color can be a great way to express yourself and define your mood. When you sit down to color, ask yourself, "How do I feel today? How can I use color to express that feeling?" Sometimes you might even feel something you can't quite put into words, but you can express it with color.

I've included some of my favorite palettes on the following page. Each one is paired with the emotion that best describes how the color combination makes me feel. But keep in mind that everyone is different, and that's what makes art so exciting. I love to use bright colors, but maybe you like more subdued colors. My "relaxed" palette might be your "cozy." There is no right or wrong when it comes to color! Use these palettes as a starting point and see how they make you feel. Try adding or taking away a color to customize the palette to reflect your taste and style. Then, make your own page full of YOUR favorite color palettes!

The next few pages contain some colored examples. You'll see two color palettes on each page, one at the bottom and one along the outer edge. The palette at the bottom shows the design's main colors in the large circles. The small circles show lighter colors (called tints) and darker colors (called shades) of those main colors. This is to give you the feeling of this palette and visually show which colors are dominant in the design (the bigger the circle, the more dominant the color).

Along the outer edge of each page, I've included a palette with each individual color, shown separately, so you can easily match your marker, pencil, or paint colors to the colors I used.

Whether you use one of my palettes or create your own, always be sure the colors you choose reflect who you are and how you're feeling.

Now go gather your art supplies—it's time to color!

The circles along the outer edge of the gallery pieces show you each individual color I used in that particular piece. If you like the palette I chose, you can use these circles to match the colors of your own pencils or markers.

The circles along the bottom of the gallery pieces show you which colors are more dominant in each design. The larger the circle, the more dominant the color. The smaller circles show tints and shades of a main color that were introduced for variety.

A SPECTRUM of Emotion

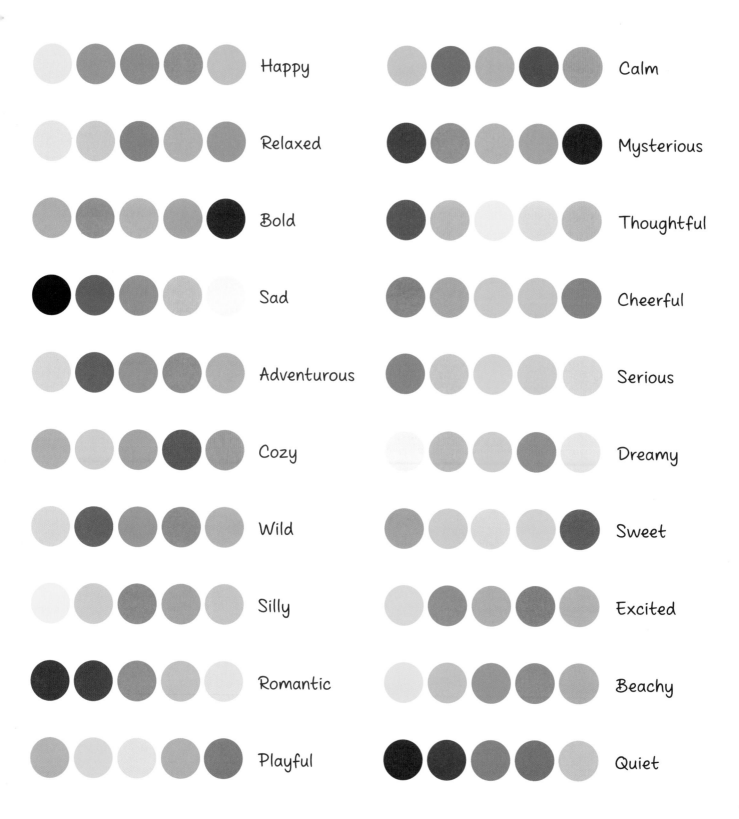

Happy

Relaxed

Bold

Sad

Adventurous

Cozy

Wild

Silly

Romantic

Playful

Calm

Mysterious

Thoughtful

Cheerful

Serious

Dreamy

Sweet

Excited

Beachy

Quiet

Take the COLOR WHEEL for a Spin!

A lot of times, simply following your feelings will lead you right to your color choices, but sometimes you might get stuck, and that's OK! Maybe you just don't know what you're feeling or you want to try something different with color and aren't sure where to start. The color wheel can be an awesome guide to help you make color choices.

The color wheel is a visual guide to the relationships between colors based on their position on the wheel. When placed together, certain colors look harmonious while others might clash. It all depends on the relationship of the colors to one another. Each color in a palette needs to be surrounded by the right companions to shine!

The Color Wheel

The color wheel diagrams below are a great starting place to find colors that will automatically look lovely together. But always remember, the color wheel is only a guide. Feel free to add more colors to a palette or take some away. The best color choices are always the ones that reflect how you're feeling and what makes you happy. Have fun!

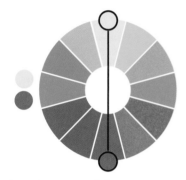

Complementary Colors
Complementary colors are pairs of opposites. They are directly across from one another on the color wheel.

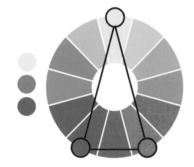

Split Complementary Colors
A split complementary color palette is created when one color is grouped with the two colors on either side of its complementary color.

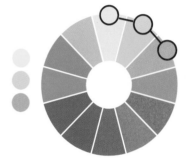

Analogous Colors
Analogous color palettes are created by choosing several colors that sit right next to each other on the color wheel.

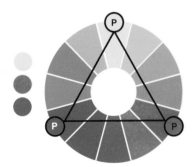

Primary Triadic Colors
Triadic means "group of three." The three primary colors (red, yellow, and blue) form a triadic palette when grouped together.

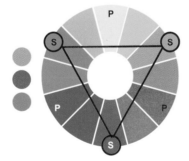

Secondary Triadic Colors
Secondary colors are the colors directly in between the primary colors on the color wheel. When you shift the triangle around the wheel by two spaces, you've found the secondary colors.

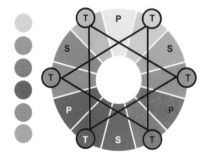

Tertiary Colors
Tertiary colors fall in between the primary and secondary colors. These are some of my favorite colors to work with!

Tetradic Colors
Tetradic means "group of four." Using a rectangle or square to choose colors on the color wheel is a fun way to instantly create a group of four colors that look great together. Both use two sets of complementary colors. Try rotating the rectangle or square around the wheel to create many different palettes.

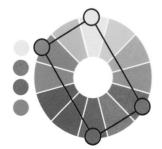

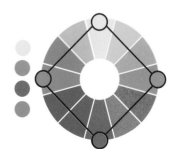

Add a little shimmer! Try using a glitter pen, marker, or paint in the white areas.

Shine on! Try using a metallic pen, pencil, or paint in the gray areas.

Make it sparkle! Try using a glitter pen, marker, or paint in the white areas.

ONE of a KIND

Try using glitter pen, marker, or paint in the white border around the star!

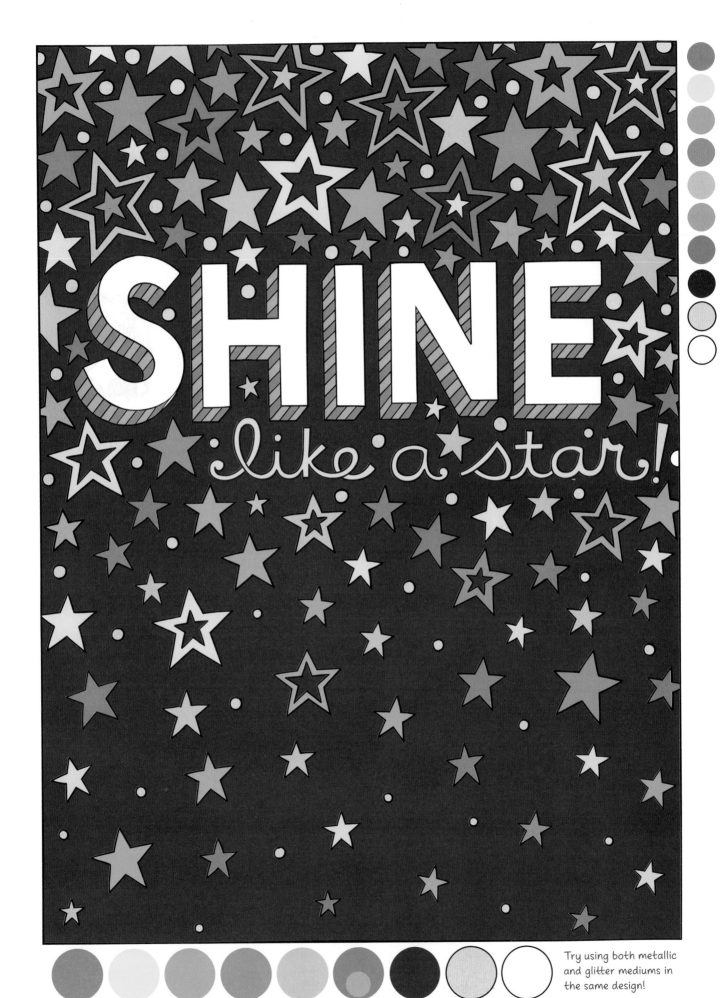

Try using both metallic and glitter mediums in the same design!

HELLO! My name is:

I feel GREAT when I:

I EXPRESS myself by:

When I RELAX I like to:

Hi, I'm Jess! What's your name? Tell me a little about yourself.

Choose four colors that are spaced around the color wheel in a **rectangle** to make your own **tetradic** color palette!

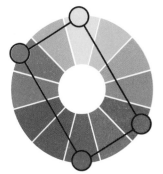

Rectangle tetradic color palette

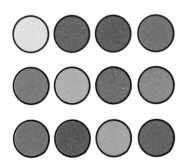

Palette examples

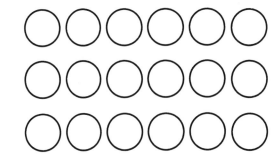

Make your own!
Also try adding a few additional colors.

The privilege of
a lifetime is being
who you are.

—Joseph Campbell

Try choosing a palette of **3, 4, or 5 colors** that are right next to each other on the color wheel to make your own analogous color palettes!

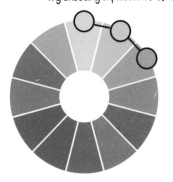

Analogous Colors

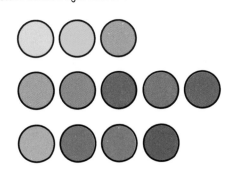

Palette examples

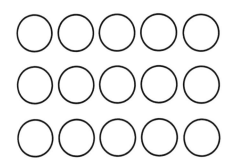

Make your own!
Also try adding a few additional colors.

Live life to express,
not to impress.

—Unknown

_____
_____
_____
_____
_____
_____
_____
_____
_____
_____

3 ways I SHiNE!

Write three ways that you shine in the stars above!

Choose **three colors** that are equally spaced from one another, making a triangle on the color wheel to create your own **triadic** color palettes!

Triadic color palette

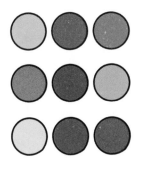

Palette examples

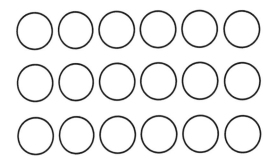

Make your own!
Also try adding a few additional colors.

Believe in yourself
and you will be
unstoppable.

—Unknown

BE BOLD

Shine BRIGHT

CREATE

REACH FOR THE Stars

follow your DREAMS

INSPIRE

© Jess Volinski • *www.jessv.com* • From *Notebook Doodles Superstar* © Design Originals • *www.D-Originals.com*

Choose **four** colors that are equally spaced around the color wheel in a **square** to make your own **tetradic** color palette!

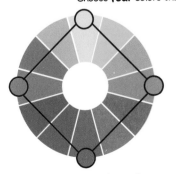

Square tetradic color palette

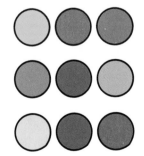

Palette examples

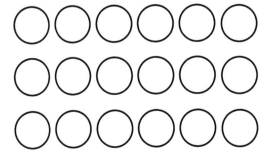

Make your own!
Also try adding a few additional colors.

Don't be afraid
of silly ideas.

—Paul Arden

Write the best advice you've ever heard in the bubble above!

Find a color you like and then choose the two colors right next to that color's complement to make your own **split complementary** color palette!

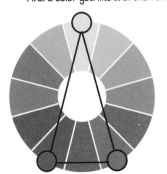

Split complementary colors

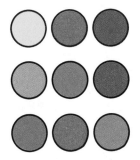

Palette examples

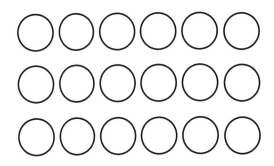

Make your own!
Also try adding a few additional colors.

Everything begins
with an idea.

—Earl Nightingale

_____
_____
_____
_____
_____
_____
_____
_____
_____
_____

Nothing can dim
the light that
shines from within.

—Maya Angelou

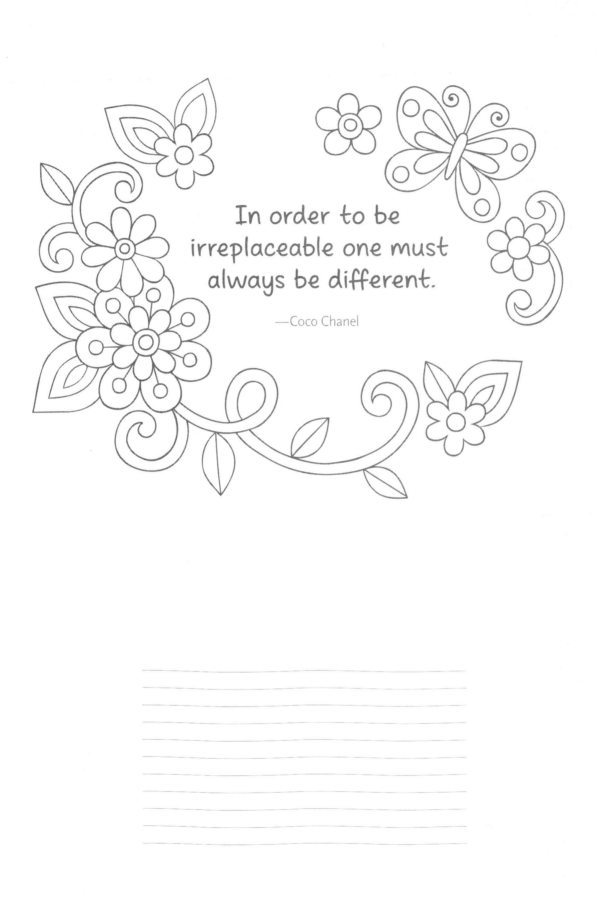

In order to be
irreplaceable one must
always be different.

—Coco Chanel

Life isn't about finding yourself. Life is about creating yourself.

—George Bernard Shaw

This world is but
a canvas to our
imaginations.

—Henry David Thoreau

10 ways I am Creative

1. _____
2. _____
3. _____
4. _____
5. _____
6. _____
7. _____
8. _____
9. _____
10. _____

List 10 things you enjoy doing that express your creativity!

Creativity is contagious.
Pass it on.

—Albert Einstein

_____
_____
_____
_____
_____
_____
_____
_____

ONE *of a* KIND

Be a star in
someone's sky.

—Unknown

Stand tall, darling.

—Unknown

Believe you
can and you're
halfway there.

—Theodore Roosevelt

Stop being afraid
of what could go
wrong and focus on
what could go right.

—Unknown

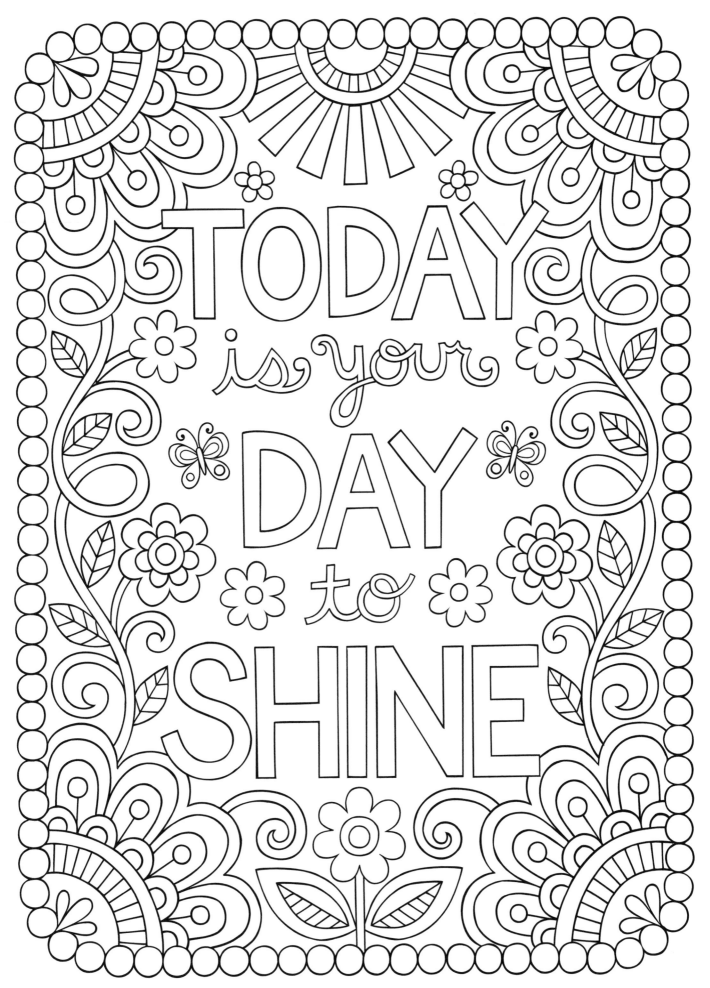

TODAY is your DAY to SHINE

If you can dream it,
you can do it.

—Walt Disney

Once you become
fearless, life
becomes limitless.

—Unknown

Everything you can
imagine is real.

—Unknown

Write or doodle about three great ideas you have for things you want to make or do!
BONUS: For each idea, list one or two steps you plan to take to make it happen.
And remember, always dream BIG!

Go confidently in
the direction of your
dreams. Live the life
you've imagined.

—Henry David Thoreau

Our greatest glory is not in never failing, but in rising up every time we fail.

—Oliver Goldsmith

Proceed as if success
is inevitable.

—Unknown

We rise by
lifting others.

—Robert Ingersoll

It's a good day to have a good day.

—Unknown

THE WORLD IS YOUR Canvas; make it a MASTERPIECE!

Follow your dreams.
They know the way.

—Unknown

You inspire me

You are better
than unicorns and
sparkles combined.

—Unknown

Create an inspiration board full of doodles, pictures, and writing about whatever inspires you most!

Every accomplishment starts
with a decision to try.

—Unknown

_____
_____
_____
_____
_____
_____
_____
_____

All our dreams can come true if we have the courage to pursue them.

—Walt Disney

Leave ❤ A LITTLE Sparkle wherever you go!

She who leaves a trail of glitter is never forgotten.

—Unknown

Happiness lies in the joy
of achievement, the thrill
of creative effort.

—Franklin D. Roosevelt

BE A Super Star

Be brave, be bold, be you.

—Unknown

YOU CAN DO IT

The future belongs
to those who believe
in the beauty of
their dreams.

—Eleanor Roosevelt